To Elai[ ]

I see a

Xmas Present

awno I've ruined it),

Norm

MODERN BRITAIN

Norman Ferguson & Mary-Claire Kelly

This book belongs to:

....

PORTICO

First published in the United Kingdom in 2008 by
Portico Books
10 Southcombe Street
London
W14 0RA

An imprint of Anova Books Company Ltd

ISBN 9781906032388

A CIP catalogue record for this book is available from the
British Library.

10 9 8 7 6 5 4 3 2 1

Printed and bound by CT Printing Ltd, China

This book can be ordered direct from the publisher.
Contact the marketing department, but try your bookshop
first.

www.anovabooks.com

www.iseemodernbritain.com

INTRODUCTION

Modern Britain: birthplace of the world wide web, binge drinking and Jude Law. Britain is a country that has seen many changes over the years, from the decline of manufacturing industries to the introduction of men sporting handbags. It is now full of things (the country that is, not the handbags) that to a person years ago would appear very strange: telephones that can be carried around, television cameras on lamp posts and young women wearing furry boots.

If there's one thing that has changed Britain it's the motor car. It's transformed the way we travel around. Over three quarters of the population have access to a car, though at times it feels a lot more, especially when stuck in a queue on a Sunday afternoon near a Swedish furniture outlet. In our cars we drive to work, drop the kids off at school, drive to a DIY warehouse at lunchtime to pick up a dehumidifier to help return sodden homes to normality, drive home, drive to the local Chinese to pick up a takeaway meal, drop off bottles at a recycling centre and, if of an adventurous mind, drive to a quiet area and watch others have sex in and around their own motor vehicles.

Our cars also take us to the shops. If Britain was once a nation of shopkeepers it's now a nation of shoppers and shoplifters. With our home-owning, latte-quaffing, gym-going, two car-owning, superfood munching, cheap flying, alcopopping, non-smoking, therapy attending, happy happy lives we have never had it so good.*

Of course cars would get nowhere if it wasn't for the people inside them, and that is one thing Britain has a lot more of nowadays: people. There are now more than 60 million inside the country and during the summer many more come to see our Goths, wheelie bins, and the London Eye. Examples of our modern way of life are everywhere. Keep your eyes peeled and your pencil sharpened and here we go!

HOW TO ENJOY YOUR I SEE BOOK

Use this book to enliven your journey around Modern Britain by identifying the things shown. As you see them tick the box and answer the questions. (Answers at the back - no peeping!) If you can complete the book, our staff will happily reward you by sending a certificate with a big "Well Done!" printed on it. Simply write to the address below, enclosing an SAE and a crisp £20 note:
I See, 10 Southcombe Street, London W14 0RA
Happy Seeing!

Apart from in the 1950s

WE LOVE OUR CARS

Britons love their cars, more than any other nation apart from the United States, Saudi Arabia, Korea, Italy, Germany, Canada and Cuba. And Iceland. However there is a special bond between a Briton and his or her motor car that reflects their drive for individuality and need for self-expression. In the past it was said an Britishman's home was his castle, but nowadays it might well be his or her car.

This car belongs to a boy racer aka 'Tree Fodder'.
I See driven round and round by drivers rarely above the age of 24

This car is for the lady who can't get enough pink.
I See Barbie's car made real

Start 'em young. Little Tikes are one of the most popular types of car a child can drive about in.
I See them not getting put away in garages for the night, but left to fade in gardens

Urban congestion needs urban congestion solutions. Despite their appearance these cars are intended for adults.
I See some smart thinking parking sideways

4

Mass car manufacturer Henry Ford offered customers vehicles in any colour, as long as they were black. Nowadays he'd probably say as long as it's silver, so ubiquitous is that colour of motor on our roads and dual-carriageways. Can you See these while heading down the highway?

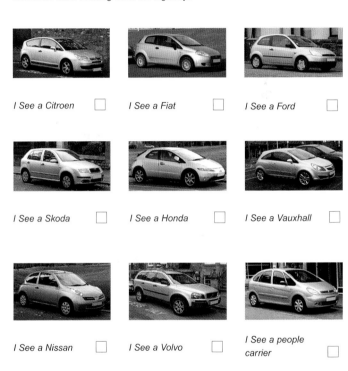

I See a Citroen ☐	*I See a Fiat* ☐	*I See a Ford* ☐
I See a Skoda ☐	*I See a Honda* ☐	*I See a Vauxhall* ☐
I See a Nissan ☐	*I See a Volvo* ☐	*I See a people carrier* ☐

I See a Toyota ☐   *I See a VW* ☐   *I See a black cab* ☐

SUVs (or "Morningside Massey Fergusons") are amongst the biggest cars in Britain. They are much maligned for being too big, too polluting, too dangerous, too expensive and sometimes being driven by people who are simply too much. With their bulky designs and height they are not difficult to See.

They are designed to go anywhere.
I See a SUV in a disabled space and not a blue badge in sight ☐

They can easily straddle any obstacle.
I See more than half in one space. Good effort. ☐

They can also easily be parked at any angle.
I See 2 wheels on the pavement, 2 on the zig-zags ☐

Despite their height and easy visibility off-road vehicle drivers can encounter problems manoeuvring in relatively small roads.

I See a 10 point turn ☐

At a recycling point.
I See blithely offloading wine bottles from halfway around the globe ☐

A rarity.
I See a SUV in town that has dirt on it ☐

WE LOVE OUR CARS

With cars becoming more nondescript, many drivers like to personalise them with signs. Some alert those behind of their precious cargo. However, signs saying a child is on board don't always prevent a shunt. Can you See cars with these and others?

I See a baby on board ☐

I See Ronnie Corbett's car ☐

I See a poorly-raised child ☐

I See God is my Sat Nav ☐

I See a Mitsubishi Evo-lution ☐

I See a clue for the police in a missing person's enquiry ☐

I See One Foot on the Clutch ☐

I See the breakdown of the reasoning approach ☐

I See a highly unlikely scenario ☐

One of the great fun things to do when out on a long journey is to make words out of the letters and numerals on car number plates. Some keen motorists have already thought about "personalising" their registration plates.

Can you guess who they are?

I See this driven by a person named Violet. Or one who likes flowers. ☐

I See Miss Kitty? Katy? ☐

I See a decorator's van ☐

I See a nice love heart for "Seona" maybe? ☐

NINA·G

I See almost a one-time Eurovision performer for GB ☐

AIO GNA

I See heart disease? ☐

NES5IE

I See a monster not coming over the hill but parked in a car park ☐

I See a driver perhaps called C Hyslop? ☐

N44RCO

I See Marco? A not-too-bright undercover drug squad officer? ☐

MIRGO

I See a Margo just one out? ☐

A TO B

In order to get from A to B, moving about on foot is still popular. As well as being good for the walker's health it also has the benefit of not burning up any non-renewable resources.

This woman has ensured she is warm enough on her walk with a hat, trousers and a long scarf.
I See a potential trip hazard when going up or down stairs ☐

This man has opted to let the skateboard's wheels move him along.
I See only a few miles an hour on this flat piece of ground ☐

Some prefer to combine walking with drinking a coffee.
I See a problem with what to do with the cup ☐

Those who prefer faster transportation take up jogging.
I See frustration, running on the spot at traffic lights ☐

A common sight in the more attractive towns is the independent travelling foreign tourist whose limited budget mean they walk everywhere.
I See rucksack, bag, camera, lightweight coat, guidebook, GPS ☐

There is nothing like sitting back and letting the internal combustion engine - or someone else - take the strain.

Here's an Australian backpacker earning some pocket money pedalling a rickshaw.
I See a fine for driving without anti-perspirant ☐

Mopeds are a small and efficient way of emulating living in Europe.
I See 50mpg, bella, bella! ☐

Many young fit professional people prefer to "push the envelope" by going mountain biking at the weekends, with their bikes perched on the roofs or boots of their cars.
I See 2 bikes at the start of the journey and hopefully 2 at the end of it ☐

Others head off to Cornwall in an old school VW camper van to surf and hopefully avoid ingesting any toxic sewage.
I See 2 weeks off if they don't ☐

A TO B

Flying can be a gigantic pain in the arse, from the frustrations of booking online, incurring 'service' charges when amending the details, forgetting your passport, queuing interminably, removing your belt to get through security to waiting for your luggage to appear. Yet despite this, millions take to the skies each year and all of them return, in some shape or form.

Here a large queue of customers are lined up trying to make their flights.
I See the last call for Flight IC123 boarding at Gate 13 ☐

A policeman patrols the concourse looking for anyone worth taking a shot at.
I See no "I've got a suspicious package in my trousers" jokes ☐

It's not all hell on earth however as duty free allows bargains to be had.
I See frequent flyers spending their airmiles on leather-look passport holders ☐

At the final destinations passengers can spend time awaiting their luggage.
I See my bags. In Barcelona ☐

While travelling by air was for many years the preserve of the rich and good-looking, nowadays many are able to fly from one airport to another with "budget" airlines. Can you name these different airlines?

This jet is "not difficult":

_____ Jet ☐

This airline rhymes with Brian Hair:

_____ ☐

Don't "be my baby":

_____ Baby ☐

These pilots should wear crowns:

_____ Air Force* ☐

*Routes are limited to Iraq and Afghanistan or any other trouble spot from around the globe.

ON OUR BIKES

Pushbikes and their riders are a common sight around the country, although the days of young lads delivering bread in large-framed bikes up steep villages are now long gone.

A parent towing their child to an exclusive primary school.
I See £500 for the bike accessory, £15,000 a year school fees, and £400,000 for a house inside the catchment area ☐

A parent with child aboard.
I See the poor mite only inches from daddy's arse ☐

A fan of Jacques Cousteau riding a small fold-up bike as a couple of workies look on.
I See wheels smaller than a pizza ☐

A low-rise bike, straight from Tomorrow's World, that allows the rider to adopt a more relaxed sitting position.
I See an eccentric in a 21st century Sinclair C5

A bike on the pavement.
I See some cyclists with no Highway Code in their back pockets

A bicyclist trying to outrun large buses.
I See a Number 10 closing him down

When out in the country be careful not to See too closely a peloton of lycra-clad cyclists.
I See far too much if they're coming towards you. Ew.

ROUND THE BEND

Driving used to be one of life's little pleasures, but these days, there are many things to turn our fun into stress. While still keeping your eyes on the road, can you See these?

Gaily painted speed cameras can be Seen brightening up any city…
I See over 30mph for a fine plus points ☐

… or out in the country where their sighting can lead to a sudden tap on the brakes by a startled driver.
I See a possible shunt up the rear end ☐

They can also be seen congratulating your adherence to the speed limits with an electronic smiley face.
I See :) mph ☐

Speed bumps not only slow you down, they can give your suspension a good testing.
I See £300 to get your front springs replaced, plus labour ☐

Average speed cameras are more common now. They divide the distance between them by the time taken by the vehicle to determine the speed, or S=D/T.
I See a higher than average rate of acceleration once past the last camera ☐

Vehicles are dissimilar from sharks in that they do have to stop at some point. When they do, it's time for councils to make revenue, whether it be via car parking charges or fines.

A woman reaches for a ticket from an automated machine at a multi-storey city centre car park that may smell of urine or worse.
I See £2.50 for 1 hour, 1 to 2 hours £4.00 and plenty of cash in the council's coffers ☐

After a short break, a parking warden races off to catch an errant motorist.
I See a frustrated Barry Sheene ☐

Oh f*@k! A motorist returns to find a parking ticket placed on his car 8 minutes after his ticket expired, despite being on a quiet residential street causing no obstruction or hindrance to anyone.
I See £60 please! ☐

This car has proved to be such a nuisance it has been removed by lorry to a pound where it can be reclaimed once enough money has been paid.
I See a cost of £105 a day plus £12 "storage fee" a day plus the original parking fine ☐

ROUND THE BEND

It's not just petty parking enforcement that drives Britons "round the bend". A lot of frustration can be derived from drivers who do what they like, where they like.

A SUV blocking a cycle and pedestrian path.
I See cyclists ending up on the bonnet if not careful

A car stopped on a cycle lane.
I See hopefully not a real cyclist underneath

A car parked on a "keep clear" space.
I See a driver who can't read

A van parked on a town-centre pavement.
I See 18 inches of space to get a wheelchair through

A large saloon car parked on a double yellow line in a car park.
I See a lazy git

A car squeezed into a space that requires passengers to exit via the sun roof.
I See Harry Houdini's car

Two cars parked right next to each other in an otherwise empty car park. Why do they do it?
I See a herd instinct, or maybe it's love

ROUND THE BEND

When out on the road, other sources of annoyance can easily be Seen. The secret is not to get mad but your I See book at the ready.

A cyclist pedalling across a pedestrian crossing at a red light.
I See two wheels where there should be two feet ☐

A queue of cars behind a slow-moving caravan.
I See your two week's holiday ebbing away in front of you ☐

Patronising overhead motorway message board.
I See safe roads everywhere ☐

A road coned off for repairs but no work persons in sight.
I See steam coming out of the ears and a BP of 140/90 ☐

A driver getting out of his car to show his frustration at another motorist in a verbal and possibly physical manner.
I See Road Rage! ☐

Long gone are the days of a workforce consisting of factory workers, office typists, coalminers and fishermen. In their place have come new jobs, or "mock jobs", with many of them not at the top of the payscale.

Supermarket home delivery van driver. The young driver's spirit having been broken by too many top floor flat deliveries of groceries involving bottled water and extra large tins of flageolet beans.
I See a charge of over £5 per delivery ☐

A ball pool cleaner.
I See 2500 balls per 2m pool ☐

Tail gunner on a helicopter in Afghanistan.
I See 7.62mm calibre tracer bullets ☐

A Polish plumber, possibly from Crackow...
I See the whole job done for £500 ☐

EARNING A CRUST

Although not renowned for personal hygiene, computer technicians have an important role to play, keeping all those computers humming away.
I See 6.5GB of SCSI IDE RAM GHZ, or something ☐

Call centre worker.
I See two minutes for each toilet break and no personal calls or chatting ☐

CCTV operator. Someone needs to keep an eye on us, and make a video compilation for their mates to watch of the best bits.
I See everyone ☐

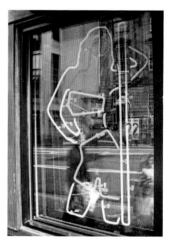

Strippers and go-go dancers used to dance around in the buff for money but have been replaced by something much more classy: lap-dancers.
I See everything for £10 but no touching ☐

With the advent of new technology there is a risk of workers developing Repetitive Strain Injury (RSI).
I See Carpal Tunnel Syndrome ☐

This line of work is not new but its place on the high street is.
I See a very long term contract ☐

Generally near the bottom of the career ladder is the forlorn person holding up a 'Golf Sale' sign.
I See Fore! pounds an hour ☐

Street charity fund raiser with clipboard ready to pounce.
I See a direct debit of £5 a month just to get them to leave you alone ☐

EARNING A CRUST

Not everyone is lucky enough to get a mock job. Others discover that working is not really for them. We all need money to exist, so alternative means of not working for a living have to be found.

This man is playing guitar on a portable amp, the proceeds going into the guitar case.
I See Oasis' Wonderwall any minute now ☐

Many see the opportunity for a long-lasting career following a stint in a reality TV show.
I See a queue of zany characters ☐

A man sits begging, ignored by busy shoppers.
I See a desultory 2p thrown in his cup ☐

This woman, who is homeless, tries to sell a copy of a fortnightly publication to another woman, who isn't homeless.
I See most people walking right past ☐

If your long-term financial plans depend on this, it might be time to consider alternatives.
I See the poverty cycle ☐

Some of those who do work can spent their day's toil far away from the cosy confines of the open plan office.

This man is collecting supermarket trolleys. *I see a wonky wheel making them a bugger to steer. How many can you See?*

_____ ☐

This worker is in a half-submerged cage collecting canal sludge to be taken away by lorry.
I See a few bad career choices along the way to get here ☐

A mini digger is being driven to the nearest roadworks.
I See the work of 20 men being done by this little beauty ☐

EARNING A CRUST

Unless you 'work' from home or are a house husband/wife, your day of work will begin with a commute. This could involve…

A long journey spent standing up, hanging off a strap in an underground train.
I See one hour of this, trying to avoid breathing in the whiff of a smelly tramp ☐

A suburban train ride followed by a race to get through the ticket barrier first.
I See no rush to get to work from those at the back ☐

A long sit in your car staring at the tail-lights of the cars queuing in front of you listening to radio bulletins advising of traffic delays.
I See that calming pan-pipes CD going on soon ☐

Crossing a busy road
like a military platoon.
*I See the 100 metre
dash before the taxis
jump the lights* ☐

Catching up on the
latest crime news with
a free paper on the bus.
*I See 35 minutes
to go* ☐

Putting make up on
while stationary at traffic
lights.
*I See should have left
more time* ☐

EARNING A CRUST

Nearing work many commuters take the chance to look like busy, successful city-types and......

...grab a coffee...
I See someone who should have got one of those holder things ☐

...grab a coffee...
I See second degree burns on one hand ☐

...or grab a coffee.
I See only another five to get my free latte! ☐

Just off the train there's time to make a quick phone call.
I See this is going to be a long day ☐

There's time to get in a coffee, a chat, and a paper before the office.
I See one of these being dropped ☐

Have a drink of orange juice in an attempt to ease a hangover.
I See it going to be a very long day ☐

Many workers are lucky enough to work in offices, protected from the elements.

Once in they can settle down to a hearty breakfast.
I See crumbs in the keyboard ☐

One of the most important parts of office life is 'skiving.' A common method is to stay seated at a desk but instead of reading emails or planning a project, to surf websites instead.
I See the average UK worker spending 57 minutes a day seeing who's 'poked' them on Facebook ☐

Here workers may face a PowerPoint presentation, with the prospect of a flipchart brainstorming "break-out" session to follow.
I See no way of checking emails for the next three hours ☐

They can also set up a hot desk in a private work area.
I See Ctrl Shift Poo ☐

EARNING A CRUST

Long gone are the days when the British would stop for a proper sit-down lunch at lunchtime. Today, most graze at their desks or nibble on the hoof. If they do actually sit down to eat, it's not at a table where knives and forks are used, but anywhere they can get stuck into whatever fast food they've bought.

…on the grass…
I See mayonnaise on your tie ☐

Lunchtime can be spent on foot…
I See mayonnaise on your jacket ☐

…or the lunch table for most: the desk.
I See yoghurt in your USB port ☐

If the morning's been too much some opt for a quick sleep.
I See drool up your sleeve ☐

At the end of the long day, or short if you've flexi time, it is time to head home.

Some prefer to stay on, to look good, and get some quality surfing done.
I See Presenteeism ☐

On the bus it's time to look depressed.
I See only the seat next to the nutter left ☐

Waiting for a train can allow time for a quick beer or 6 with a colleague.
I See 21 units for men per week, not per night ☐

On the train the repeated rhythm of wheels on track can lead to a small nap.
I See 40 winks before Tooting Broadway ☐

Once home it's time for some executive relief.
I See Busty Commuters III ☐

And then off to bed.
I See a 6.00am rise ☐

PASSING THE TIME

Not every waking hour in Modern Britain is spent working: some lucky people have the chance to spend some quality time doing things they enjoy. Can you See yourself doing these activities around Britain?

Getting a bird's eye view of a capital city on a gigantic ferris wheel called an "eye."
I can See someone breaking into my car from here ☐

Trailing round a large Scandinavian homeware warehouse at the weekend.
I See a flat-pack nightmare ☐

Queuing up to withdraw your lifetime's savings from a bank on the edge of financial collapse.
I See interest lost due to waived 90 day notice of withdrawal ☐

Protesting about the loss of terms and conditions at your workplace.
I See a final salary pension, when do we want it? Now! ☐

Baying at an alleged criminal.
I See a lynch mob ☐

Taking the dog out and collecting its poo in a bag.
I See picked up pooch poop ☐

Some like to get their kicks from more hazardous pastimes, such as...

Tumbling down a hill in a transparent ball, or "sphere", at 30mph.
I See £50 a roll (with a no liability clause in case of accident or injury) ☐

Pot holing in a twisted labyrinthian underground network of caves.
I See dem bones dem bones ☐

Calling a policeman a big fat plod.
I See size 10s bearing down on your soft bits ☐

Risking psychosis by over-indulging in mind-altering drugs.
I See Class A, B or whatever, man ☐

PASSING THE TIME

With its northerly latitude, Britain gets its fair share of night-time. This allows many opportunities to pass the time nocturnally.

You can protest against a debate involving pro-fascist speakers.
I See 1933 all over again ☐

Queue up to buy the latest computer game equipment.
I See 1 Wii per person ☐

Lie down on the street incapacitated by drink.
I See PC Kronenbourg 1664 on hand ☐

Send a poor quality version of a music gig to a friend, in real-time.
I See many arms aloft ☐

Or just stay in front of your computer into the wee hours.
I See the days merging into each other ☐

For the ultimate in pastimes there is nothing like an outdoor music festival. These are now held up and down the length of the country during "summer". If you like chilling out with your friends, drinking expensive alcohol from a plastic cup and seeing the same bands over and over again then the music festival scene is for you.

Glastonbury.
I See some hippy moaning it's not what it used to be ☐

T in the park.
I See few cups of Earl Grey and no cucumber sandwiches ☐

Leeds Festival.
I See the same bands. But in a slightly different order. ☐

V Festival.
I See the Arctic Monkeys? Oh no, it's the Magic Numbers ☐

Being outdoors, festivals can fall foul of the weather.
I See a scene familiar to survivors of the Somme ☐

One of the Must See events of any festival is the queue for the portaloos.
I See holding it in until Monday ☐

JOIN OUR CLUB

Everyone in Modern Britain is an individual, although with close-knit Neanderthal tribes in our genetic make up, it's understandable that we sometimes club together in groupings whether formal or informal. Keep your I's peeled for these clubs.

A group of men on a night out - possibly a stag night - with no jackets.
I See shirtsleeves in sub-zero temperatures ☐

A giggle of unapproachable, well-groomed, professional women drinking white wine in trendy city centre bar wondering why they're single.
I See another bottle of house white for table two ☐

A swally of gnarly tramps drinking on a bench.
I See that's my can you fugger you, here gie's it, it's mine ☐

An aileron of aviation enthusiasts photographing at an airshow.
I See an EOS 100-400L
f 4.5 /5.6 at 400 ISO ☐

What is an affectionate name for aviation enthusiasts?

_____

A lager of football fans dressed as crusading knights.
I See 3 Lions on a Cloak ☐

A trebuchet of battle re-enacters.
I See Mordor, 1415 AD ☐

A pride of gay people dressed up on a parade.
I See PC 69 on duty ☐

JOIN OUR CLUB

Skateboard kids sit chatting missing a neat trick by a fellow boarder.
I See an ollie kickflip, dude ☐

A pair of Goths slip easily between the living world inhabited by most of us and the other world.
I See Bela Lugosi's still dead ☐

Brightly dressed girls stand around catching up.
I See Converse, Converse, Converse, Dunlop, pumps ☐

Group of boy teenagers sitting around in hoodies. They're not causing any trouble but cast fear into every old person's heart by their presence.
I See National Service for the lot of 'em ☐

Similarily-dressed girls wearing big boots last seen worn by cold grannies.
I See me with all my frahnds, yah? ☐

Hen night participants wearing pink bunny ears meeting some young men.
I See a few drinks then an early night.
Ahem. ☐

Weekend biker on a large motorbike
I See 1200cc of pure fuel-injected road power.
Vroom vroom! ☐

At an ancient stone monument carrying out some rites of ancient pagan religion.
I see far out druids communing with the spirits of the ancient world, until 10.30 when a bus party of German tourists arrive ☐

39

JOIN OUR CLUB

As the population ages and health provision improves, Modern Britain is becoming increasingly full of old people. But, despite their numbers, they pose little threat to the rest of the population, unless you dare stand quietly in front of them when it's their bus or there's only one bag of mint imperials in the shop. They can be Seen…

…in a lay-by soaking up the rays…
I See Sun Protection Factor 0 ☐

…on a bench…
I See I'm 87 you know ☐

…at bus stops…
I See nothing coming, now where have I put my glasses? ☐

…at a train station.
I See Platform 65 for a free travel pass ☐

One group of individuals that are commonly Seen on the streets and country lanes of Britain are the well-to-do students or "rahs". Most university towns will be familiar with the tousled "bed" hair, large sunglasses, short skirts, scarves, and large furry boots. And the women dress bizarrely too.

With a chum in jogging bottoms.
I See Casual Rahs ☐

Here's one, with a chum, up town.
I See Big Boot Rahs ☐

On their own.
I See Cold Rah ☐

What they will grow into.
I See Grandrara and Grandrara ☐

41

UNIQUE BOUTIQUE

People in Modern Britain like to wear nice clothes, many bought from boutiques or supermarkets. As much as is possible Modern Britons try to create an individual look, while still looking the same as everyone else. Those with an eye for fashion can See these in the urban jungle.

Here's a metro sexual male.
I See him with a man-bag ☐

With a Bluetooth headset plugged in ☐

A 'Nathan Barley', probably a web designer and part-time DJ.
I See hours of preparation to look like you got dressed in the dark ☐

A tattooed young lady, the tattoo signifying her affection for her partner.
I See Dave, 4 eva ☐

A man pulling his suitcase while listening to tunes on his round-neck headphones.
I See tinnitus and beers at four ☐

Tall man with long coat, hair, beard, and wearing cowboy hat and boots, striding.
I See this town ain't big enough for the both of us, pardner ☐

Slightly scary man in combat gear but not actually in the army.
I See one in every town ☐

UNIQUE BOUTIQUE

A woman wears training shoes to prevent wear and tear on her work heels.
I See fifteen minutes moderate exercise a day ☐

And here's a man doing the same.
I See that nine o'clock dropping right off the radar ☐

A Scotsman.
I See nothing worn under the kilt - it's all in perfect working order ☐

A young man walking his scary dog in area of social deprivation on his bike.
I See leisure wear ☐

Adult male with trousers hanging round his arse riding a too-small BMX bike.
I See his pants ☐

A protestor handing out leaflets with ubiquitous "protest" head scarf.
I See an end to capitalism, poverty or whatever else needs sorting this week ☐

A teenager who admires those non-macho men interested in technology.
I See The Geek Hearter ☐

SPLASH THE CASH

Britain is a nation of shopkeepers, and this means just about anything can be bought or sold. Shops are the main mechanism for such transactions, whether they are in malls, or high streets, although the internet is fast catching them up.

This one sells mucky videos.
I See lots of brown paper bags ☐

This shop sells Scottish souvenirs to tourists and has a hilarious name.
I See rugs for a fiver, that'll do nicely! ☐

Fireworks at cheap prices.
I See 12 super rockets, 14 turbo blasters and 6 sparklers for let's call it £5 ☐

This large supermarket is open morning, noon and night and sometimes later.
I See 2 for 1, or 3 for 2, or 6 for £5. With a clubcard. ☐

SPLASH THE CASH

It is wrong to say malls are cathedrals. Try getting a burger in St Paul's. No, malls are self-contained mini high streets with fixed roofs so shoppers need never see rain or daylight. Originally from America, they are now a permanent part of the British out-of-town landscape. Can you See these around the country?

Trafford Centre, Manchester.
I See 280 stores under one roof ☐

Metro Centre, Gateshead.
I See 500,000 visitors a week ☐

Designer Outlet Centre, Livingston.
I See 400,000 square feet of retail space ☐

Meadowhall, Sheffield.
I See 30 million visitors a year, and most of them here this afternoon ☐

Their car parks can make it difficult to find your car. What lane is it in?
I See Level 2, Blue area, row E. Or was it J? ☐

There are plenty of opportunities to grab some tasty fast food.
I See £1.99 a meal big deal ☐

POLSKI SNACKS

The incorporation of extra countries into the European Union meant many more eastern Europeans could come to live and work in Britain. Like all nationalities abroad they missed the small things in life in the way British people miss Tunnocks' Teacakes, brown sauce and curries. To meet this demand many shops "catering" to these new palates have opened up.

Polski Smak.
I See slaska sausage ☐

Polish shop.
I See tymbark juice ☐

Polski Sklep.
I See podwawelska sausage ☐

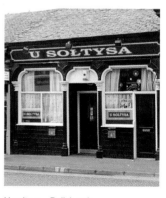

U soltysa - Polish pub.
I See a pint of Tyskie, please ☐

46

CHARITY BEGINS IN THE STREET

Charity shops can be Seen in every high street in every town in every county up and down and across the land. If you don't mind the cramped layout and unalphabetised book sections there are many bargains to be found, assuming the online traders haven't got there first.

Kidney Research.
I See a man's grey suit, hope no-one died in it ☐

Cancer Research.
I See an ashtray for a pound ☐

Barnardos.
I See crash barriers probably not needed ☐

Shelter.
I See no Big Issue seller ☐

British Heart Foundation.
I See no wristbands - whatever happened to them? ☐

PDSA.
I See Ace Ventura: Pet Detective video for fifty pence ☐

Bog standard Oxfam.
I See five fair trade sandalwood joss-sticks for a fiver ☐

Oxfam - this one sells only books and music.
I See a first edition Harry Potter for £7 grand ☐

Oxfam - this one is a Supersaver branch.
I See what next - a loyalty card? ☐

PINK THINGS

In the post-feminist, post-modernist world, manufacturers are keen to re-emphasise women's femininity by offering many different items in one colour: pink. It's the new black.

This car comes in many colours but for the gal about town, pink is the colour.
I See pink furry dice ☐

This computer will work just as well as a boy's, though it might not visit the same websites.
I See www.boysare stinky.com ☐

An mp3 player.
I See whose new album?
_____ ☐

This phone hasn't had collagen implants.
I See Lesley Ash recoiling in fear ☐

This is a Gameboy, for the game-playing girl.
I See Britney Karaoke ☐

The phrase "To feel good, you have to look good" is often heard nowadays. Not everyone can be as good looking as Trinny or Susannah however, but that doesn't stop us trying.

One way of feeling good about yourself is by having Botulinum toxin injected into your forehead.
I See a permanently surprised look ☐

Another is to keep an eye on your body mass index. Machines are thoughtfully provided in various locations, including public toilets.
I See a BMI of over 30, fatty ☐

Another is to have your chest size increased - pecs if you're a man, breasts if you're a woman. Many celebrities have "had their's done".
I See a cupsize bigger than her head ☐

Surgery can often be painful and while it might not be too appealing on a wet day, exercise can also help.
I See a speed walker ☐

BOTOX NATION

Money can't buy you love but it can buy you better looks. Splash out on the following...

This razor allows a very close shave.
I See 5 blades, where there might be room for 7, or a hundred, one day ☐

A good haircut can make all the difference and can be had in this salon.
I See a little something for the weekend, sir? ☐

Or in this punningly-titled salon.
I See a punter getting confused over a blow dry and set ☐

This cream attempts to halt the march of time.
I See Dorian Gray in no need of the painting in the attic ☐

The most important thing is to remember what it's all about.
I See me me me ☐

Most people live in flats or houses with very few inhabiting houseboats or caves nowadays. Modern homes take many shapes and forms, and with land at a premium any space will do for building properties.

This housing estate of individual properties sits not far from a busy main carriageway.
I See only a few minutes drive until the road rage starts

This estate sits next to another estate, currently being built.
I See the kids playing at Cowboys and Builders

Some houses are built near to areas that flood easily in bad weather.
I See George Alagiah in wellies

These flats sit next to a rail line.
I See the 6.00 am from King's Cross acting as an alarm

Many singletons or couples choose to buy expensive executive flats with a tiny balcony large enough for a pot of jam.
I See a single bedroom flat with 2 toilets

GRAND DESIGNS

Those who live in glass buildings shouldn't throw stones. If that's the case there will be few being thrown in Modern Britain. Offices, flats, shops, greenhouses all use this transparent building substance. Many offices in particular use glass but while it might look good, workers have to shut the blinds to prevent glare and so any benefit in having lots of viewing potential is lost. Argh.

A municipal authority's headquarters.
I See 10 wonky floors shaped like a snail's shell ☐

A museum.
I See 315 tonnes of glass triangular panels ☐
How many can you See in the roof? _____

Here's an office building with many different tenants.
I See 8 floors with some capacity unutilised ☐

Another office complex.
I See a phallus-shaped vegetable ☐

The Victorians were great exponents of the "We need that sort of building, so we'd better build it" approach. With public funds not so readily available following the demise of the tea, opium and slave trades, nowadays if a building is needed, an old one is converted, particularly if a public art gallery is required to display piles of bricks and other masterpieces of contemporary art.

Tate Modern, London.
I See an ex-power station ☐

Baltic, Gateshead.
I See an ex-flour mill ☐

Tate Liverpool, Liverpool.
I See an ex-warehouse ☐

Gallery of Modern Art, Glasgow.
I See an ex-library ☐

GRAND DESIGNS

Church buildings are used for a number of purposes.

The classic antiques showroom conversion.
I See a pair of brass candlesticks for £80. Cheap as chips! ☐

A social work centre.
I See no alms for the poor but lots of forms to fill in for benefits ☐

This ex-church is now home to a number of swanky flats.
I See a different kind of conversion ☐

Some are even used for religious worship.
I See The Vicar of Dibley waddling along at any moment ☐

There is no point in having a lovely house and it looking like a relic from the 1990s or worse: the 1980s. One of the simplest ways that house owners ensure their homes look good is by visiting large furniture warehouses and fitting out their domicile with the co-ordinated products available.

Bookcase.
I See an Aripotta ☐

Chest of drawers.
I See a Braandpantyi ☐

Sofa.
I See a Larrdass ☐

Bed.
I See a Slobbi ☐

For that final flourish, many install laminate flooring, a simple and effective solution to not having it.
I See the flat below hearing every foot step

BLOOMING GARDENS

Despite the inclement weather, neighbours' loud music and a location under a flightpath, Britons like to enjoy their gardens.

Part of the gardening experience involves a trip to a garden centre where you can get a scone, a cup of tea and a Busy Lizzie for a not unreasonable sum.

I See three geraniums for under three quid ☐

A piece of pre-shaped topiary can help bring some fun to a garden.

I See 3 saying Fore! ☐

Wind chimes can bring a sense of tranquillity and peace. Though not always to a neighbour kept awake by their incessant clattering on a windy night.

I See Britain's Worst Neighbours on channel 234 at 9pm ☐

Decking is a simple way of not having to cut grass.

I See a low maintenance garden ☐

BLOOMING GARDENS

Some keen horticulturists prefer to grow their plants indoors, especially these hemp plants, which can help arthritis sufferers or people who have trouble giggling.
I See a trip to the law courts ☐

A decent-sized leylandii can help keep nosy neighbours from looking into your garden.
I See vitamin deficiency from lack of sunlight ☐

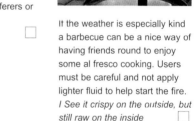

It the weather is especially kind a barbecue can be a nice way of having friends round to enjoy some al fresco cooking. Users must be careful and not apply lighter fluid to help start the fire.
I See it crispy on the outside, but still raw on the inside ☐

Bumble bees are not seen as often as in the past and their gradual disappearance could lead to a global food crisis for mankind.
I See the end of humanity ☐

IN THE FAMILY WAY

Such are the joys of Modern Britain that people want to have children to share the fun with a new generation. There are a wide variety of ways to transport the wee mites around, some able to cope with the north west face route up Everest.

I See a child lying almost completely flat in this all-terrain orange mega buggy ☐

I See dad with one on the floor, one in the plastic car and one in the shopping basket ☐

I See protection from rain, sleet and fresh air ☐

I See a portable car-seat and potential back trouble for mum ☐

I See a top-of-the-range buggy carrying the toilet roll home ☐

I See baby sick in mum's hair ☐

I See a four-wheeled, front-mounted, aluminium and nylon mobile family unit ☐

I See a young man with pram anxiously looking for his mates ☐

While families are not as large - in terms of numbers - as they were, there is no doubting the pride that parents have in their offspring. They can be Seen interacting with them in different ways.

A dad attempts to talk to his children who are engrossed in their games consoles.
I See whatever, dad ☐

This family have been dragged out into the freezing cold air for a walk.
I See a MacDonald's to buy them off ☐

This dad laughs at a text while pushing his child along the street.
I C u l8r m8 ☐

Here's a young mum at the bakers with her buggy.
I See 2 hot sausage rolls and a pasty for breakfast ☐

A middle-class parent reasons with her tantruming child.
I See a sir or madam being spoilt ☐

IN THE FAMILY WAY

With the career safely parked, many parents devote themselves to a new project: having a child. This effort is replicated when they come up with names, all of which are officially registered and not made up, honest.

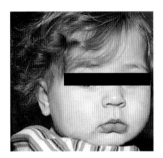

This one could be called Chanelle…
I See a reality TV career ☐

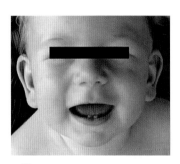

…Che…
I See a poster on his bedroom wall ☐

…Kobain…
I See him being kept away from the shotgun cupboard ☐

…Merlin…
I See a round table ☐

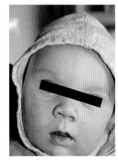

…Treasure…
I See where X marks the spot ☐

…Seabastian.
I See a typo at the Registry Office, or a fondness for an ocean-going fish ☐

Keeping hale and hearty is difficult in our busy lives so to make sure our health is up to scratch many pop a pill, rub on some ointment or spray on some chemical help.

Garlic pills will maintain a healthy heart and ward off Vampires.
I See 0.049g of polyvalent alcohols per tablet ☐

Milk thistle is not a fluid produced from a lactating Scottish weed but is for repairing an over-indulged liver.
I See 45mg of Silybins. Whatever the hell they are. ☐

As few Britons now get scurvy, many take Vitamin C to boost their immune systems and ward off colds.
I See this one counting towards my five a-day portions ☐

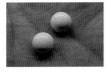

These tablets can bring relief from worry and anxiety.
I See no storing above 25 degrees C ☐

Why not kill all birds with one multi-vitamin pill? This one to be taken orally.
I See 120mg of Omega-3 or maybe just a jellybean ☐

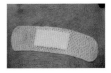

This plaster is silver-enriched and so will not only aid healing but make you feel like a million dollars.
I See platinum corn plasters next ☐

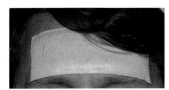

Headache pads.
I See looking like a patient in a World War I sanatorium ☐

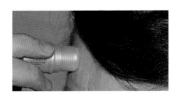

If all else fails why not rub this pain relief stick on your forehead?
I See minty bliss ☐

REGULAR AS CLOCKWORK

Moving your bowels on a regular basis is as important to long-term health as taking exercise or buying a kidney from a Third World resident down on his luck. Nowadays there are more advanced methods to keep us "on the go".

A healthy start to the day is a nice bowl of a bran-based cereal. Some prunes on top and there will be no stopping you.
I See never mind a Number 2, this could be a Number 3 ☐

This yoghurt is specially formulated to help improve digestive transit.
I See not the most appealing of advertising slogans ☐

If these natural methods fail, it's time to get the tubes and the warm water out.
I See mushrooms ☐

If too much "digestive transit" is experienced there is no need to panic.
I See the modern solution: take a pill ☐

A MENTAL STATE

It's not only bowels that have to be working well in Modern Britain. Our minds also need to be in tip-top condition. Pressures of modern life and too much daytime television can turn a brain into mush unless it's cared for properly.

Counselling can be a useful method of gaining insights into what troubles us. If nothing else you get to talk about yourself for hours on end.
I See our time's up already. Unless you want to pay for another hour? ☐

If mental strength requires more…unusual methods, healing crystals are very popular. They have unique properties and if it floats your boat then what the hell, it's your money.
I See a load of crystal balls ☐

Staring at candles and thinking is highly recommended by some for producing a stable mind. Unless your candles are next to curtains or fabric wall hangings.
I See a fire engine on emergency call-out ☐

Failing that, many swear by angels who can provide guidance and spiritual calm.
I See Luke Chapter 1 verse 11 ☐

MODERN BUGS

Older style illnesses such as diphtheria, polio and smallpox are no longer fashionable in Modern Britain. Hopefully, these modern diseases will not be Seen too often.

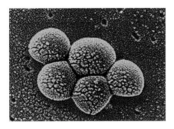

MRSA.
I See a bug that is anything but super ☐

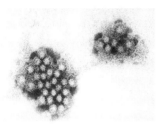

Famous for appearing on cruise ships it's the winter vomiting bug or Norovirus.
I See it sounding far more impressive than just 'flu' ☐

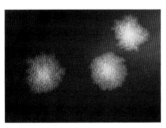

C Difficile.
I See a hospital in dire need of some Dettol ☐

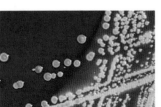

E Coli.
I See in retrospect that burger was a mistake ☐

Allergies are becoming increasingly popular in Modern Britain. Famine, pestilence and war brought on severe reactive symptoms to Britons of old while nowadays it's more likely to be wheat, dairy milk and non-precious metals.

It is often joked that some people are allergic to hard work. But it's no laughing matter if this leads to a build up of bed bugs which can cause irritating bites...
I See Cimex lectularius. Are you tucked in comfortably?

...and an increase in asthmatic symptoms.
I See one in eight children wheezing away

Peanuts can bring on allergic reactions, but some producers make sure any nuts are labelled with a notice saying "Contains nuts".
I See 100% nuts

HOME CLEAN HOME

With many now living in homes not kept clean by mother or salaried servants, keeping a house tidy is not easy. The last thing anyone wants to do after a hard day's work is come home to a hard evening's work.

Some hire a cleaner.
I See a homeowner working out with the cross-trainer and not a vacuum cleaner ☐

Others are content to let dust bunnies collect on wooden floors.
I See plenty more nasties in the carpet. You just can't see them. ☐

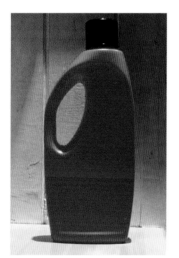

And if all else fails, one way of trying to prevent disease spreading is using an antibacterial hand washing gel.
I See 99% of germs wiped out. Until they develop immunity… ☐

As with so many other things, the solution can come from a bottle, as in this sink and plughole unblocker.
I See in case of contact with eyes, seek medical help immediately ☐

NATIONAL HEALTH SERVICES

It's harder and harder to be healthy, with many obstacles to achieving a sound mind and body.

Dental work is not so easy to get, with private treatment becoming the norm.
I See a queue near a dentist's accepting NHS patients ☐

If you are careless or unlucky and catch something not pleasant in your "personal area" you'll need to visit a building like this.
I See now called a GUM clinic, not a VD one ☐

Gyms are expensive and being surrounded by fit and healthy people can put off the fatties, so much so that £200million a year is wasted on gym memberships not used.
I See £120 a month ☐

Having a knockabout game of footie can be hard, as there's no-one to play with.
I See empty playing fields on a Saturday morning ☐

Of course you can be the healthiest person in the world and still trip up on a computer cable and break your neck.
I See a breach of health and safety in the workplace regulation 1102/B paragraph (3) ☐

SAVE OUR KIDS!

Children are the future and our most important assets, even surpassing pets in the eyes of some. There are many ways to keep them safe from the dangers of Modern Britain.

...or reflective jackets when crossing the road.
I See them a mile off ☐

One way of ensuring their protection is for mum and dad to get them a slash-proof school jumper...
I See stab-proof nappies next ☐

To find where they are you can put a GPS tracker unit in their jackets.
I See where they are but not what they're up to ☐

Next step: put a microchip under their skin.
I See the future ☐

You can never be too safe and a child should wear a crash helmet when sitting in a field.
I See those daisies could have an eye out ☐

Another good method of securing their safety is putting a sign on a bus acting as a timely reminder for parents…
I See them probably in their rooms on the internet ☐

…or on an ice cream van.
I See a 99 flake and a choc-ice, please ☐

To let them roller-skate without any protection apart from clinging to the fence should be a criminal offence.
I See jail or a birching for those parents ☐

Also effective: driving them to school in mummy's SUV.
I See a street full of the feckers ☐

READING AND RITING

Children can avoid the soul-destroying wastelands that are the sink estates if they secure a good job with great prospects. There is very little mucking about in class as school children compete and scrabble to get the highest possible results.

They are continually assessed and constantly having to write down what they know in exams.
I See x being the square of y when f minus z is the product of the Battle of Hastings ☐

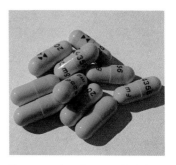

Stress can play a large part in their lives. Especially if their myface page doesn't get as many visits as it used to. This can lead to the prescription of Fluoxetine hydrochloride.
I See 2 a day with a glass of water ☐

With a culture of no-one is a loser, exams are there for everyone.
I See A+ A+ A+ A+! ☐

Despite all the effort some mistakes can creep through.
I See only one letter out ☐

The internet has been a revolution for youngsters. Whereas before they would be criticised for hanging around outside now they get dog's abuse for spending all their time indoors. Who'd be a kid, eh?

Children nowadays learn computer skills at younger and younger ages.
I See a password: ma-ma ☐

Teachers have to prevent them downloading their essays off the net.
I See exactly the same mark for all ☐

One of the worst aspects of the Internet Age is the possibility of children being groomed by dirty old men on chat rooms, where grooming means something different than combing a horse.
I See some believing castration is too good for them ☐

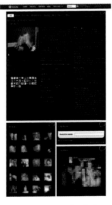

Social networking is all the rage.
I See no-one over 40 understanding it at all ☐

DOGS ARE A CHILD'S WORST ENEMY

Despite dogs being equipped with sharp teeth, strong jaws, powerful bodies and the occasional need to hunt prey many families keep dangerous breeds of dogs as pets. Even the quietest of Sunday walks can be transformed into a panic-ridden experience for a child if a supposedly "friendly" dog jumps up on them and gives them a life-long fear of the smelly mutts. Can you See these drooling and snarling about the place?

Staffordshire Bull terrier.
I See Zuul from Ghostbusters ☐

Argentinean Dogo.
I See the Andrex puppy has been working out ☐

Bull terrier.
I See no-one laughing at the birthmark on his ear ☐

CCTV cameras are on every corner of Modern Britain, to protect us from both terror attack and from each other. They are never used to film people peeing, having sex or stumbling about drunk for the amusement of the operators, which can be sent to *You've Been Framed* for an easy £250.

See them...

...in a rural town's high street...
I See no one at all ☐

...at the seafront...
I See seagulls ☐

...at a road junction...
I See people peeing up lanes at night ☐

... in a car park with the additional feature of a loudspeaker...
I See cars parked ☐

...inside, on a stairwell...
I See broken lifts ☐

...at a climate change protest on a very long tower...
I See crusties ☐

... in a cage...
I See the last couple getting smashed up ☐

...in a bus...
I See fare dodgers ☐

...cunningly disguised in a police van.
I See a riot of colour ☐

SIGNS OF THE TIMES

Essential for any well-ordered society, determined to ensure high levels of health and safety, is the sign. It can warn us, tell us what to do, or tell us what not to do.

I See glowing in the dark

I See Kenny Loggins' on the mp3 player

I See puzzled looks at this outdoor no smoking zone

I See death. Or a tickle under the armpit

I See someone walking into the sign

I See some right dingbats out there who can't work out how to operate a trolley

I See budget restrictions at the local council

I See no confusion here about whether you should enter or not

I See overhead cables. Somewhere...

I See hot water that may be very hot ☐

I See no doubt about water temperature here ☐

I See Evel Knievel's trademark 'warning-triangle' jump stunt ☐

I See a hot drink that's hot. Whatever next? ☐

I See people just breezing in willy nilly ☐

I See an average of 14 a year ☐

I See gaffer tape in an expensive building ☐

I See most rivers being unfenced ☐

I See a fine worth many pints of lager ☐

REFLECTIVE JACKETS

Health and safety guidance recommends wearing reflective garments where possible when out and about. They can now be Seen everywhere. So much so that pretty soon those not wearing them will stand out.

I See loose and casual attire ☐

I See full-length high-visibility jacket and peaked cap ☐

I See no problem being Seen in this longer garment ☐

I See a civilian in a neat and tidy outfit well-fitted ☐

I See waistcoat and hard hat worn over long sleeves ☐

I See Ali G in a full high-viz outfit. Aii! ☐

I See a man warning others of his chronic flatulence ☐

I See two outfits that scream "safety" ☐

I See co-ordinated safety outfits at the train station ☐

One of the more unpleasant aspects of walking the dog is cleaning up its mess. Before, the muck could be left lying until someone touched it and became blind, or worse, got it all over the clothes their mum had just washed. Thankfully, authorities have provided plenty of signs to stamp this out.

Here's how to do it, by using a shovel in Angus.
I See jobby be gone ☐

You could use your hands in East Lothian.
I See a huge pile of doggy mess radiating microwaves ☐

Some advise catching it straight into the bag on this wall-mounted bin.
I See good luck with that ☐

It's a Health Hazard.
I See a steaming pile ☐

In Gateshead it's a £1000 fine if your dog fouls.
I See a large cigar ☐

In Harrogate it might be your dog in the dock.
I See woof justice ☐

NO SMOKING

Smoking is the greatest sin in human history and offenders are lucky not be punished by a period in the stocks. Whatever the pros and cons you can still See smokers out and about.

This man is enjoying a smoke al fresco.
I See 77,000,000,000 cigarettes smoked each year in Britain ☐

A list of ingredients of this packet of cancer sticks.
I See no smoke without hydrogen cyanide ☐

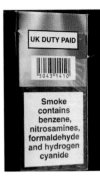

UK DUTY PAID

5043 1410

Smoke contains benzene, nitrosamines, formaldehyde and hydrogen cyanide

These gentlemen are having a lovely draw in doorways, sheltering from the fresh air.
I See less than £2billion spent on smoking-related illnesses in the NHS ☐

This is a canopy for visitors to have a puff and not get soaked.
I See £8billion collected in tax revenue each year ☐

There is much to be scared of in Modern Britain: disease, gangs, property price crashes and the return of the Cybermen, amongst many others. Here is a selection of fear-ridden things to keep a careful eye on.

Having a large picture of a magnified virus and a headline such as that may lead to the very thing it's advocating against.
I See a bit of a panic ☐

News bulletins give the latest traffic, weather and crime reports.
I See Penny with the latest from the Old Bailey ☐

This newspaper board keeps us on our toes.
I See Stranger Danger at the front door ☐

With so many diseases around, it's best to wear one of these at all times. Not just during sex.
I See them ribbed, flavoured and multi-coloured. Maybe better wear two just to be safe ☐

Policemen are there to protect the public by shooting terror or crime suspects.
I See reassurance ☐

SCARED BRITAIN

Many young people wear a casual hooded garment called a "hoodie". While most are harmless, some are far from it and you can never be too careful.

Hoodie alert! They are dangerous no matter the age.
I See trouble ahead ☐

I See a hoodie up to no good walking down the street ☐

This pub sign keeps them out.
I See a nice safe pub ☐

This newspaper board tells us all we need to know about what they are capable of.
I See the bringing back of public flogging ☐

This hoodie top is spelt: f.e.a.r.
I See David Cameron coming, arms outstretched ☐

There is plenty to See when out and about on a day trip or stuck in traffic. The eagle-eyed will be able to See these and much more.

A trolley far away from the confines of the supermarket car park.
I See someone's ride home last night on the way back from the pub ☐

Unfortunately some of our animal cousins don't survive their contact with our modern world. Has anyone ever Seen a live badger?
I See 50,000 badgers a year run over on British roads ☐

A burnt out car in a field.
I See 3rd party, fire and theft ☐

Some of our human cousins don't survive contact with the natural world and they are commemorated by their loved ones with bundles of flowers tied or nailed to trees, fences or lampposts.
I See over 3000 human road deaths a year ☐

What else can you See when out on the road?

A plastic carrier bag in a tree.
I See 10 billion bags used a year ☐

A deflated child's helium balloon in a tree.
I See an atomic number of 2 ☐

A family having a picnic lunch in a car park.
I See fish paste sandwiches for everyone and some mineral water for the dog! ☐

A burger van in a lay-by.
I See a fried egg roll please, luv ☐

There's no effort required to see prehistoric Stonehenge which conveniently sits next to the A344.

I See a 5000 year old visitor attraction. For free. ☐

The Angel of the North, outside Newcastle, is also easily seen from a number of major routes.

I See a Number 21 bus for a perfect view ☐

The large distinctive shape of wind turbines can be seen all over the country.

I See 1 bird killed per turbine per year ☐

OUT AND ABOUT

As well as the more popular sights there are other attractions to be Seen for those with a keen eye.

An encampment of travellers beside the sea.
I See council officials arriving to move them on soon ☐

A car park that looks innocuous during the day but at night could be awash with doggers.
I See 8 months suspended sentence and a couple of years on the sex offenders register ☐

This road sign has been altered to say something rude. Tee hee.
I See Buckstone Gardens missing some ink ☐

As has this one.
I See it standing proud for weeks for all to see ☐

A new addition to the landscape is the mobile phone mast (MPM). They can be seen poking up into the sky anywhere and everywhere. Do they emit dangerous rays? We simply don't know. I See free weekend calls and minimum 12 month contract for each:

Carefully painted to look like a lamp-post… ☐

… standing quietly in the corner of a farmer's field… ☐

…on a pavement next to a car garage… ☐

…in a supermarket car park… ☐

…gathered together on a municipal building… ☐

…on top of a football stadium ☐

OUT AND ABOUT

News used to be posted up on town walls for locals to read. With TV and RSS feeds this is no longer necessary but there is still some information given out in this way.

I See a diva inscribed on a hand rail at a tourist viewpoint ☐

I See action. Now, people! ☐

I See writing that is short and curly ☐

I See a cheap date ☐

I See some wag writing 'she is' underneath ☐

I See a frosted bobby attempting to have intercourse with an ice cream or is it a snowman? Or even a ghost? ☐

I See a cash machine enlivened by an interesting scatological drawing ☐

Public artworks Seen up and down the country can bring some fun and thoughtfulness to our streets. Some of it is publicly funded by the taxpayer or lotto player, while other artworks are self-financed.

A town attempting to win a Britain in Bloom competition can have floral bouquets draped round the town.
I See a plaque for "Best Hanging Basket Above a Bin" ☐

This public artwork is a set of steel tubes arranged together to turn the wind into music.
I See 70,000 scratchcards paying for this baby ☐

No town centre statue of a renowned figure is complete without a traffic cone thrown on top of their head.
I See students ☐

Anarchists take matters into their own hands with this installation piece called "Smashed up bus shelter".
I See no laws, yeah ☐

This figure on a plinth allows a suitable resting place for these London pigeons.
I See the pigeons offering their own critique ☐

Satellite dishes provide a tidy flourish to any row of flats.
I See UK More TV 3+1 Extra Gold ☐

STAY OUT!

To enjoy the countryside fully there are many obstacles to overcome. However you may be lucky and avoid any contact with the Countryside Alliance. What else is there to See?

Ramblers getting in the way all over the shop.
I See Janet Street Porter ☐

A sign telling you to keep out.
I See no welcome mat at this farm ☐

A Blue Tongue outbreak.
I See a pink one for now ☐

A foot and mouth outbreak.
I See pyres, buckets of disinfectant and a lengthy ban on British meat ☐

FOOD GLORIOUS FOOD

Britons love their grub. So much so that despite the best efforts of certain TV chefs, obesity is, like love in the 1960s, all around us. Literally, in some cases.

Smoothies are a quick way of getting those vital fruit vitamins inside you without any of the bother of peeling or cutting up fruit. Buying them also means you don't have to go through the pretence of buying fruit and letting it rot in your kitchen.
I See 5 portions a day. And possible indigestion. ☐

Healthy food not sold by those beastly supermarkets can be bought at a farmer's market.
I See one every month on the 3rd Saturday, 9.30 til 12.30 behind the church ☐

Not so healthy food can be pushed through a school railing by your mum however.
I See Jamie Oliver not getting his message through ☐

It's essential we have all the information to make an informed choice. Even a chocolate bar tells us what we need to know.
I See only 14.6g of fat in this 49g bar ☐

Be treatwise - Get to know you			
EACH BAR CONTAINS . . .			
Calories	Sugars	Fat	Saturates
255	27.8g	14.6g	9.1g
12.8%	30.9%	20.9%	45.3%

. . . OF YOUR GUIDELINE DAILY AMOUN
To be enjoyed as part of a healthy 1

COFFEE CULTURE

One of the biggest changes in our eating and drinking habits is the rise of binge-coffeeing. We just cannot get enough coffee, whether it's a tall skinny latte, a double caramel mochafrappalatachino or a tiny espresso.

Coffee can be had anywhere. This woman is enjoying hers while walking her dog.
I See a Yap-achino ☐

This café is positioned next to an urban shopping centre.
I See how many empty chairs? ☐

If you fancy an al fresco cup of Joe, this table has been thoughtfully placed and cordoned off for your exclusive use.
I See a bus lane right there, and free exhaust fumes with your mocha ☐

This kiosk is for those on the move.
I See one bored student "barista" paying off his student debt ☐

Superfoods are amazing. As well as giving us essential minerals, proteins and riboflavins, they also thin the blood, heal the sick and create worm-holes allowing time and space travel.

This month's flavour of the month is the goji berry.
I See £15 a kilo ☐

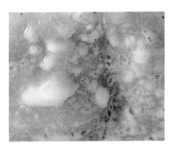

It's claimed oily fish will help our hearts and make our children more cleverer. Instead of giving them homework, teachers now take them fishing.
I See Omega-3 oozing from every fish pore ☐

Blueberries are a superfood because of their high levels of anti-oxidancy. They are supposed to help prevent ageing and, combined with cream and a nice pastry base, also prevent anyone not having a yummy dessert.
I See a helluva lot of yum here ☐

Oats are one of the superest of superfoods. However, some like to add maple syrup to taste. With maybe a bit of sugar sprinkled on top. Oh and with full-fat milk.
I See 11g dietary fibre per 100g for all the good that'll do ☐

ECO WORRIERS

As well as the TVs, video recorders, DVD players, digiboxes, hi-fis, digital radios, telephone answering machines, wireless routers, computers, games consoles, printers, scanners, lights, cookers, microwaves, food processors, juicers, washing machines, dishwashers, fridge freezers, toasters, breadmakers, espresso machines, irons, hairdryers, curling tongs and vacuum cleaners that run off mains electricity in the house, we also use many other items that burn up energy. Can you See these in Electric Britain?

A laptop can be recharged with this cable.
I See 3 hours worth of charge ☐

Mobile phone charger.
I See 3 hours of chat time ☐

A car.
I See 48 miles of travel, but less if the cable snags ☐

A marital aid.
I See 20 "ah-ah" multiple orgasms per AA battery ☐

An electric hand towel dispenser.
I See the height of laziness ☐

Rather than go to the bother of pushing open a door, many press the button of these electrically-operated doors designed for the disabled.
I See new ways of using up electricity ☐

RUBBISH BRITAIN

With the Wombles now retired, Britain is in danger of turning into a gigantic bin.
Can you See these on the streets?

A fast-food container in a canal.
I See a houseboat for a rat □

A park covered in rubbish.
I See Great Uncle Bulgaria turning in his grave □

It's not surprising there's so much stuff lying about when products come with excessive packaging.
I See something in the box, oh yes there it is □

A discarded fish and chip wrapper □

A tasty morsel being fought over by some pigeons □

A dog's pee □

RUBBISH BRITAIN

All sorts of things get thrown out of our houses. Some of them make it to the bins or council special uplift trucks but a whole lot more are just dumped.

A mattress.
I See 29million tonnes of household rubbish collected each year ☐

A mattress and a couple of monitors.
I See 25% of household waste recycled ☐

A painted bust of Michelangelo's David.
I See 10% of waste burned in incinerators ☐

Not the kitchen sink but a bathroom toilet.
I See 509kg of waste per person per year ☐

All manner of crap left by a field.
I See rubbish on moi land! ☐

Fast food containers.
I See £424 worth of food thrown out each year ☐

Luckily there are people around who are able to take care of some of the mess. When in town can you See these?

I See a high pressure job ☐

I see two women starting the week by washing away god knows what from outside their work after a weekend ☐

I See a waste-disposal engineer demonstrating his expertise ☐

I See the best method of cleaning up autumn leaves is hiding them under a roadsweeping truck ☐

STINKING THE PLACE UP

Like a wet tramp in a bus, humans are in danger of smelling up the place something rotten.

A landfill site.
I See 16.9 million tonnes of landfill each year and about the same number of birds ☐

A car's exhaust contains bad things.
I See CO, CO_2, N_2, H_2O, NO_x and maybe some $H_2C(OH)_2$ ☐

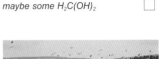

Central heating exhaust.
I See steam belching outside but a warm and cosy house inside ☐

Aircraft contrails left in the sky can make for pretty patterns but can form clouds to increase the greenhouse effect.
I See phew, what a future scorcher! ☐

Patio heaters outside a pub. Being cold is nature's way of telling you to go inside or put on a jumper.
I See over 2 million of the things bought so far and 4 tonnes of carbon dioxide a year ☐

USE IT, RE-USE IT

Tears for Fears said that everybody wants to rule the world, but away from the hedonistic 1980s we all want to save the world: recycle, re-use and re-re-re-flex. Or was that a song by Duran Duran?

We now wash not only our dishes and cutlery, but also the food containers.
I See beans on a drying rack ☐

Our houses are littered with boxes of cardboard, plastic, tins and cans and newspapers.
I See a trip hazard ☐

We see nothing wrong with driving our petrol-fuelled motor cars and SUVs to Recycling Centres, but that's because it's great fun to throw stuff into a big bin and hopefully make a loud noise.
I See a trip in dad's car every Saturday ☐

Or we can wait for a large diesel lorry to come around and collect our stuff for us.
I See a 20 tonner ☐

Plastic bags have a bad name now and the ethically-minded can be seen taking their shopping bags to the shops. A bit like older people have been doing, forever.
I See 1 bag per person ☐

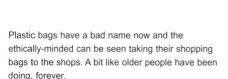

WHEELIE BINS

A new addition to the street furniture of Britain is the wheelie bin. These high density polyethylene waste containers can be Seen everywhere.

I See a Continental 660 ☐

I See a green one, outside a scotch whisky club ☐

I See a brown recycler WBD 240 ☐

I See two black OMB 3280s ☐

I See three purple Heavy Duty 240 litres ☐

I See five Four Wheeled 1100s covered by tasteful blue covers ☐

I See a Bradshaw Electric PC40 ☐

I See a burnt-out OMB 3280 ☐

I See seven WBD 240s awaiting the lorry ☐

As the land area of Britain gets smaller due to coastal erosion, we risk losing space as other things become bigger.

Fast food can be had very early in the morning which, combined with a low level of exercise, can result in weight being put on.
I See 246 people per square kilometre ☐

Once people stop smoking, weight can be gained.
I See an average of 6 to 9 pounds gained ☐

Cars are also getting bigger, with the Mini being more like a Maxi.
I See a width of 1.69m ☐

The original Mini was a lot smaller.
I See this one being about 5cm wide ☐

One product seems to be reversing the trend and appears to be getting smaller.
I See more like your fat fingers getting fatter, fatties ☐

WE CARE

The best way to show how much you care is to only buy products that are ethically, ecologically and morally right on.

Cleaning products that don't burn baby fishes' faces with their acidic bleach.
I see the planet slowly r-ecover-ing itself back to health ☐

Only purchase your gifts from an ethically-correct shop.
I See a lot of lentil soup ☐

Only drink coffee that is ethical, honest, fair, ethical and honest.
I See 1 World ☐

If it all gets too much, get plastered on swally that has been traded fairly.
I See 14% of saving the planet goodness ☐

A more simple method of reducing our carbon footprint may be needed: the mass suicide of the human race. With all humans gone the carbon footprint of the race would be much reduced. Failing that, in the future the best things to do are learn to live without…

…cod for our fish suppers…
I See eating Brill, Bream, Coley or Dab instead ☐

… petrol for our cars…
I See pushbikes and horses making a return ☐

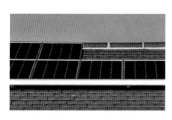

… roofs without expensive solar panels.
I See rainwater used in the toilets too ☐

Once we have passed on we must ensure our remains are composted.
I See ashes to ashes, dust to dust, us to flowerbeds ☐

BOOZY BRITAIN

With the stresses and strains attached to living in Modern Britain it's unsurprising that so many like to take their mind off things with a big drink.

Alcohol can be tempting. Especially at these cheap prices.
I See a cheap way to a nasty hangover ☐

And it's so bright and shiny too.
I See pretty colours, like a liquid rainbow ☐

With modern transportation on hand it's even easier to get to the pub.
I See no need for a taxi home ☐

Once out you may meet a young lady and with enough booze courage indulge in a charm offensive.
I See a beautiful modern retelling of Cinderella ☐

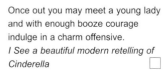

Clubs have more than disco music and lights. You could get doused with foam.
I See damp-smelling clubbers ☐

If you're on a stag night you could get a nasty weal from being shot while paintballing.
I See a real pain in the neck ☐

You could be converted by an anti-drinking campaign.
I See The Island of Dr Moreau ☐

You could have a special report on your leisure habits by serious news TV.
I See Boozenight investigates ☐

GULLIBLE BRITAIN

There are plenty of people out there waiting to take your money if you show the right level of naivety.

I See 24 hours a day psychic cover ☐

I See 2.4 children ☐

I See 3 Free futures! Incredible! ☐

I See dead people ☐

I See 7/2 Lucky Lad, 10/1 Luckier Lad, 33/1 Lucky Fecker ☐

I See the chances of it being you about 14,000,000 to 1 ☐

I See 1 in 200,000 chance of becoming a millionaire. House! ☐

I See that missing word as being 'Wasteof' ☐

I See one part water to 1,000,000,000,000,000, 000,000,000,000,000 parts water ☐

WHAT AMERICA DOES

America is like the big brother in a poor family. Once he's finished with something he'll pass it on as a hand-me-down. Can you See these around the country?

I See a large motorhome bigger than your own house ☐

I See a drive "thru" fast food outlet ☐

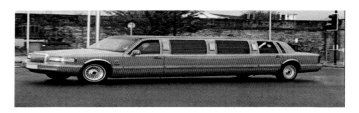

I See a s t r e t c h e d l i m o ☐

I See Prom nights ☐

I See gun crime ☐

KEEP IN TOUCH

Mobile phones are a common sight on our streets, cars and train carriages. A boon to some, a gigantic pain in the hole for others, there is no sign of us not keeping in touch.

Can you See these mobile phoners?

Once a place to spend your 2p pieces and a penny.
I See perspex ruins ☐

I'm on the train! ☐

I'm with the bairn! ☐

I'm not on the bus yet! ☐

I'm on the bus! ☐

I'm with the dog! ☐

I'm on the beat! ☐

I'm in the kiosk selling newspapers! ☐

I'm on the steps! ☐

I'm past the bins! ☐

I'm in the park! ☐

I'm in my parka! ☐

I'm in my duffel coat! ☐

I'm in my dotage! ☐

I'm in the road! ☐

I'm running across the road! ☐

I'm in my suit! ☐

I'm in the bus shelter! ☐

KEEP YOUR DISTANCE

Despite humans being natural social animals many of us can't be bothered interacting with others and prefer to remain in our own worlds.

The most popular way of keeping out the big bad world is the portable mp3 player. This allows any walk to be enlivened by an electronic soundtrack wired straight into our lugholes. Whether this results in an epidemic of tinnitus and long-term hearing damage remains to be Seen. Or heard.

Some like to read a good book while on the move
I hope I See any dog mess before I stand in it ☐

I See 200 gigabytes of downloaded trax wired right in ☐

Headphones that are normally seen plugged into a hi-fi.
I See 20,000 hz of frequency response ☐

Earphones normally seen near a hi-fi, but on a hat.
I See a man about to walk into a lamp-post, because he's feelin' the music. Ouch. ☐

There are some aspects of life in modern Britain that can cause a raised eyebrow or a furrowed brow of confusion.

Although racial stereotypes and assumptions have been challenged over the years since slavery and the emancipation of those slaves it is still possible to see some evidence of a certain non-Politically Correct worldview.

I See golliwogs for sale ☐

With dog theft on the rise a loving owner can opt to know the exact location of their dog
at any time.
I See micro chips under Rover's pelt while he's getting a shampoo and set ☐

When out having a busy day shopping or strained from the pressures of work many men like to visit a "sauna".
I See it full of bankers ☐

LOOK TO THE SKIES

When out and about in Britain there is much to be seen in the skies above.

I See a Heart-Shaped Cloud ☐

PHOTO CREDITS

All photographs by the authors unless specified.

SXC:*Round the bend:*Average speed camera-Chris Chidsey;*Earning a Crust:*Computer user with wrist support-Leonardo Tote;*Passing the time:*Recording gig with mobile-Piotr Ciuchta;*Join our club:*Pride march-speedym,Druids Stonehenge-Ted Rosen;*Botox Nation:*I love myself badge–Robert Aichinger;*Grand Designs:*British Museum-Benjamin A Ward,Gherkin-Andreas Hunziker,Garden decking-Christopher Howard,Barbecue on fire-Martin Boose;*In the family way:*Baby-Anita B Patterson,Baby-Cynthia Turek,Baby-Helmut Gevert,Baby-Csontos Lea,Baby with cap-Helmut Gevert;*Hale and hearty:*Cleaner vacuuming-Muris Kuloglija Kula,Computer-Christian Sherratt;*Save our kids:*Microchip-Hugo Humberto Plácido da Silva,Roller blader child holding onto railing-Vicky S,Bull terrier-Monika Leszczyƒska;*Out and About:*Wind turbine-Wagner Christian;*Eco Worriers:*Big modern Mini-Simon Bérubé,Old Mini-Per Evers,Cod-Niels Boegh,Empty fuel gauge-Helmut Gevert,Solar panel on school roof-Fabienne Winkworth;*Gullible Britain:*Homeopathy-tinpalace.

FLICKR:*All photographs licensed under a Creative Commons Attribution licence,unless specified otherwise by the photographer. A to B:*Bicycle Police hassling rickshaw-Malias,VW Camper in Cornwall-Jayniebell,Heathrow queue / Policeman-Heather Gruber,Duty free-Lucas Worcel,Baggage carousel-Gareth Simpson,RAF C-130J-James Gordon;*Round the bend:*Road sign speed smiley-Niklas Höglund,SUV parked in front of cycle and people lane-Peter Miller,Volvo parked on cycle lane-Janet McKnight,Road rage-Tom Hall;*Earning a Crust:*Gunner in Afghanistan-Olly Lambert,Computer technician-Jesus Angel Hernandez de Rojas,,Golf sale man-Richard Cocks,Underground commuters standing-underground.blogspot.com,Lunch at desk-Kai Hendry,London commuters having a drink-Peter Morgan,Underground commuters sleeping-London-underground.blogspot.com,In bed-Danny Williams;*Passing the Time:*Large furniture warehouse-Yusuke Kawasaki,Northern rock queue-James Holloway,Unison protest-Daniel Dainty,Policemen grabbing protestors-Dave Morris,Anti-nazis protesting-Alex Harries,Queue at midnight to buy Wii-

Laurence Livermore,Man in front of computer at night-Jason Rogers,Glastonbury-Matt Becker,T in the park-Michael Gallacher,Leeds-Ian Wilson,V Festival-James Hay,Flooded Glastonbury-Peter Burgess,Festival toilet queue-Gavin Stewart,*Join our club:*Men in shirts-Kevin Sutton,England fans as crusading knights-Andrew Burke,Hoodies-David Sim,Hen night-Kevin Sutton,Elderly sunbathers-James Laurence Stewart,On a bench-Ben Scicluna;*Unique Boutique:*Woman with tattoo-Malias,Protestor handing out leaflets-Dave Morris;*Splash the cash:*Sex shop-Malias,Trafford Centre-David Bolton,Meadowhall-Andrew Green,Pink laptop-Mistie Gao;*Pink Things:*Ipod-Zachary Antolak;*Botox Britain:*Gillette Fusion-Naotake Murayama;*Grand designs:*London city hall-Chris Brown,Tate Modern-Sergio Piquer Costea,Tate Liverpool (Mihal Orela),GOMA Glasgow-DieterM,Interior bookshelf-Divya and Deepak,Bedroom / Bedroom bed and shelf units / Living room-Raquel Peterson,Wind chimes-Rie H,Bee-Marilyn Peddle;*Hale and hearty:*Colonic irrigation sign-pj mac,Crystals-Toshihiro Oimatsu,Angel-Richard Smith,Nuts packet-Malias,Queue-Ade Oshineye,Gym-Danielle Murphy;*Save our kids:*GPS-Derek Hatfield,Boy in field with crash helmet-Kerys,Exams-Cristi Carlstead,Prozac-Aaron M Jones / Liquid7,Baby on computer-Brandy Cumberland,Staffordshire Bull terrier-Gemma Longman/www.flickr.com/photos/g-hat/,Argentine Dogo-Ricardo Martins;*In a right nanny state:*Mobile CCTV-David Hands-Clarke,River sign-Robert Brook,Alcohol restriction sign-Gene Hunt,Harrogate dog poo sign-James Cridland;*Scared Britain:*Bird flu newspaper-Jon Nicholls,Hoodie baby-Jessica Merz,Sign outside pub-Malias,Sandwich board-David Lisbona;*Out and about:*Dead badger-Jonas Bengtsson,Car park lunch-Kamyar Adl,Stonehenge from a car-Donabel and Ewen at Flickr.com,Car park-Donabel Alves,Singing ringing tree-Dave Leeming / www.calydel.com,Smashed bus shelter-John Pannell,Public art and pigeons-Gaetan Lee,Private property sign-Tom Wardill,Ramblers-Tom Maloney,Cow-Mike Colvin;*Food Glorious Food:*Farmers market-Sheila Ellen Thomson,Burger and chips-Jess Lander,Goji berries-Phil Brown,Omega 3-Bart Everson,Blueberries-Chris Gladis,Oats with maple syrup-Brad Haynes; *Eco Worriers:*Electric car charging-Frank

PHOTO CREDITS / ACKNOWLEDGEMENTS

Hebbert,Flytipping-Tim Herrick;Contrails-yaaaay,Burnt out wheelie bin-Jonathan Jones,Creme eggs-Andy Wright;*Boozy Britain:*Brightly coloured alcopops-Ian Wilson,Newcastle night out-Andy Wright,Foam party nightclub-Will Ellis,Paintball welt-Danpeng1;*What America Does:*Prom night-Ian Martin,Gun crime scene-Andrew Green;*Keep in Touch:*Policeman on mobile-David Hands-Clarke.

FreeDigitalPhotos.net:*In a Right Nanny State:*Red Dog poop bin-FreeDigitalPhotos.net.

WIKI COMMONS:*A to B:*(Aircraft) bmi baby / easyJet / Ryanair-Adrian Pingstone;*Passing the time:*London eye-Adrian Pingstone;*Grand Designs:*Garden centre-Adrian Pingstone;*Hale and hearty:*Dust bunnies–Stromcarlson;*Scared Britain:*Policeman with machine gun-Adrian Pingstone.

CDC:*Hale and Hearty:*MRSA-Janice Carr,Norovirus / Clostridium difficile / E Coli-CDC,Bed bug-Piotr Naskrecki.

Department of Justice:*Grand Designs:*Marijuana indoors-Department of Justice.

RA FERGUSON:*We Love Our Cars:*SUV parked across lines / blocking pavement / recycling;*Round the Bend:*Van parked on pavement;*Grand Designs:*Topiary golfers,Leylandii;*In a Right Nanny State:*Motorbike road sign;*WTF:*Gollies.

DN FERGUSON:*Save our Kids:*Clearence sign.

BLADE RUNNER:*Save Our Kids:*School jumper.

MAGNUM:*Earning a Crust:*Executive relief-Peter Marlow / Magnum Photos;*Hale and Hearty:*Counselling-Peter Marlow / Magnum Photos.

ALAMY:*Passing the Time:*Unconscious man-© Les Gibbon / Alamy;*In The Family Way:*Tantrum child with parent-© Sally and Richard Greenhill / Alamy;*Save our Kids:*School run-© Shaun Finch / Alamy;*Reading and Riting:*Student Celebrations-© Tim Cuff / Alamy;*Out And About:*Foot and mouth-© Agripicture Images / Alamy.

Istock:*On our bikes:*Cyclists-Angel Herrero de Frutos;*Earning a crust:*Plumber-Lisa F

Young,Call centre worker-David H Lewis,CCTV operator-Dr Heinz Linke,Toilet worker-Johannes Norpoth,Late worker-Gaby Jalbert;*Passing the time:*Plastic ball rolling-Chris Turner,Skeleton in cave-Hr0N0FaG;*Join our club:*Women drinking-Bob Thomas;*Grand Designs:*Flooding-Barry Crossley;*Save our Kids:*Computers in class-Chris Schmidt,Man on computer- Henk Badenhorst;*Out and about:*Burnt out car-Andrew Martin Green;*Keep in touch:*Mobile phone on train-Franck Camhi,Mobile phone on bus-Tomaz Levstek;

GETTY:*Passing the time:*Angry crowd.

All efforts have been made to ensure credits are correct at time of printing. Any omissions or errors in accreditation should be notified.

ACKNOWLEDGEMENTS

The production of this I See book would not have been possible without the kind assistance of those who gave up their time, energy, images and ideas. Without them this book would be poorer, although any criticism of its quality and content should not be laid at their door, but at that of the author's. Special thanks go to: Tom Bromley at Portico who Saw it early and to everyone else at Portico for making it happen; Sandy Buchanan who is generous to a fault; Debbie Strang of Whitenoise Creative Limited who took away a lot of the Quark Fear; RA and DN Ferguson who supplied images we couldn't get; HB Ferguson who had her name in two books and now has it in four; Joseph and Briana Kelly and Shona Laird for being willing models; friends and family who when told about it gave great support and encouragement, especially Linda Kelly and also PJ and Philomena Kelly; Andy Bollen without whom the Give Up option might have been taken a long time ago. Thanks must also go to the photographers of Flickr and Stock.xchng as well as Wiki Commons, whose willingness to take great photographs of all subjects and release them for creative use has been invaluable.

Answers
A to B: easyJet, Ryanair, bmibaby, Royal Air Force; Earning a Crust: 8 trolleys; Join our Club: planespotters; Pink Things: pink; Grand Designs: 3312 panels; Coffee Culture: 16 empty seats.